I *wish* I was **the**person I'M PRETENDING to BE

ALSO BY JACK GARDNER
'WORDS ARE NOT THINGS'

# I wish I was the person I'm pretending to BE

TRANSFORM YOUR PERSONAL AND PROFESSIONAL LIFE
AND BECOME THE PERSON YOU REALLY WANT TO BE

BY JACK GARDNER

## foulsham

London • New York • Toronto • Sydney

# foulsham

The Publishing House, Bennetts Close,
Cippenham, Slough, Berkshire, SL1 5AP,
England

ISBN 978-0-572-03402-3

Foulsham books can be found in all good bookshops
and direct from www.foulsham.com

A CIP record of this book is available from the British Library.

Designed by Room 7 Limited Advertising and Design.
T +44 (0) 1460 234790
www.room7.uk.com
www.wordsarenotthings.com
Printed in Great Britain by Cox & Wyman Ltd, Reading.

# BE THE PERSON YOU REALLY WANT TO BE

Relationship crap? So what are you going to do about it?
Only one option: leave you behind and become
the new you, you want to be.


Rubbish job? Are your managers incompetent?
Good, it is a damn sight easier to get where you want to be
with incompetent managers than good ones. Good managers
make you feel valued and help you achieve satisfaction from
your job. Bad ones, now they make you scream, scheme,
kick ass, lie, back stab and be unproductive, in other
words ambitious. Now we're getting somewhere.


Do not kill/get rid of a bad manager;
they will only be replaced with an equally incompetent
one or, heaven forbid, a good one.


This book will help you to transform yourself and make your
personal and professional lives successful and satisfying.
Pretending to be someone is not a vice, it is essential. After
all, our outward connection to the world and other people is an

invented or evolved state, a product of the much-discussed nurture or nature and the things that have happened to us as well as simply our desire to be a particular type of human being. How many bishops have you heard being oh so pious and talking in that soft saintly voice? How many footballers have you heard talking in that clipped, limited vocabulary: 'a penalty was really out of order'? How many policemen have you heard talking in that precise legalese? They all constructed themselves in ways that said: this is who I want to be.

Clearly much of our interaction with the world is through language, with all the limitations that can bring. Mishearing, misunderstanding, overhearing, not hearing, lies, half lies, irony, inference - the words to describe how we can misunderstand meaning in language are numerous. We struggle to force who we think we are, that person in the mirror, into the mould of who we want to be, that elusive superhuman sometimes glimpsed, never confronted.

In my first book, 'Words are not things', I wrote, 'Look inward for the most distant view'. Here in my second, I am giving you the means to do just that.

Use this book to help transform yourself
and make your personal and professional
lives successful and satisfying.

You know who you want to be,
now let's get on with it.

# Define success
## before seeking it

You curse and bluster and thrash around
but maybe that is all you want:
to appear to be a wanting, dissatisfied soul

# Where possible, aim for a bruise, time after time

Everyone has a weakness.
Find it. Exploit it ruthlessly

# 'I don't know'
## is the right answer
## to most questions

# but

## the least used

*Don't guess at answers.*
*Either you know or you don't*

# Answers
## exist before
## the questions
## they answer are
# asked

Do not fake surprise.
Find your natural expression of surprise

# You cannot
## identify a liquid by looking
# at it

Many times in life we make decisions
based on too little information

# Make sure your hands agree with your mouth

Do not underestimate other people's ability to see through your bullshit

# It is easier to think like a bear than to think like an otter

Do not assume an understanding of another person just because you sense familiarity

# Seeds can miss a year and still grow

A good idea still needs its right time

# Doing comes before thinking

A genuinely spontaneous gesture or remark
is priceless at the right moment

# Thinking hard achieves no more than thinking soft

Thinking is a tool. Learn to use it as a carpenter learns how to use a saw

# In the dark, a light going out attracts as much attention as one coming on

Be certain of the effect you are trying to create and its consequences before attempting it

# Now is the
## consequence
### of everything that
# has
### ever happened

Every moment is potentially
an ending or a beginning or both.
Which of the three is a conscious decision

# Understanding
# is not
# the same
# as knowing

To understand a person you have to know them.
To know a person you don't need to understand them

# A qualification is an admission of many ignorances

Sometimes say 'I don't know' when you do know; an excellent communications exercise

# Specialise in the general

Know only obscure information

# An idiot who knows he is, is wise, a genius who doesn't, is ignorant

Use as many tests as possible to quantify your exact mental abilities and accept the results

# A small piece of fish is small to us, but not to the fish

Make sure you know other people's list of priorities before you open your mouth

# Nature does not negotiate

Be aware of the things you really cannot influence

# Kneel in the freezing river all night and pray for the happiness of frogs

Undertake utterly pointless tasks with enthusiasm

# Your
## Will will
## be read

Imagine the room in which your will is being read.

Look from one face to the next.

Who are the people you don't know?

# If you enjoy being kind, it is selfish

Be constantly aware that doing the right thing should be enjoyable

# Success is measured

# by

## achievement not
# money

Who do you admire, I mean really admire?
If they had another million pounds
would you admire them more?

# You need your glasses
# to
# repair your spectacles

Seeing is a two-stage process. There is seeing as a mechanical function of eye physiology. Then there is seeing as in knowing. Know the difference

# Death is not a symptom

Listen to people's voices. Learn to recognise the difference between what is final and what is not

# Grains of truth are the most irritating sand

Choose a day and on that day tell only
the absolute truth about everything,
and no half truths either

# Thoughts are put in the post with no address on the envelope

Be open to the idea that a random thought might be the solution to a problem without an obvious connection between them

# The
## wise have unlearned
# the most

Think what a burden would be lifted if you could not know all the things you don't need to know, and what space would be left for wisdom

# When confronted

# by a

**bear you do not speculate**

# on its age

An ability to see danger in any situation is vital.
Do not deal with the unimportant.
Deal with the danger

# Now was

## once your destiny

It is true, you blazed a trail here across the universe to meet with destiny, but destiny has already moved on so get after it

# The higher the bridge, the narrower it looks

Put a plank between two bricks on the ground and you can walk across it backwards. Put the plank a hundred feet in the air and... Think how easy most things are if you just keep them on the ground

# A clock will give you bad advice on when to eat

Rid your life of routine. Listen to your body for when you should eat, piss, sleep and work and be prepared for surprises

# Most enemies get you with a weapon that you have given them

Always listen to your words before speaking and look at the faces of the people you are saying them to

# Shout
## when alone, whisper
# when
# in company

It is hard to hear yourself when alone,
easy when with others

# Do not look at the light, look at what it is illuminating

Rabbit, look at yourself and ask 'why?'

# Insecurity is a natural state

# of

# readiness

Insecurity, mildly, all the time, is better than sudden bouts of fear

# Now can only ever be now

Always be in the second that is happening now.
Feel it constantly

# Thoughts in the head are not words in the mouth

Beware. People use words as if the gaps between them were filled with telepathic communication

# Courage is a word, fear is a feeling

Do not mistake words for feelings. Just because you use a word doesn't mean you have the feeling

# You
## do not need a
## boat to deliver
# water

Do not speak just for the sake of it.
Stay silent, draw back into the shadows

# What frightens us the most is knowing that there are no ghosts

Identifying the source of your fears is an essential skill

# The
## neverness of
## forever

Think about the huge, unresolvable,
unknowable subjects in great detail

# The lower the sun, the longer the shadow

Be conscious that we are surrounded by all kinds of information that we often do not see

# Fear the swordsman

# with

# no sword

Use the skills you have,
not the ones you wish you had

# Questions
## are
### rarely asked
#### just to acquire information

Questions are a legitimate way of making a
statement as long as you are aware you are doing it

# A mistake rarely
## tells you something you
## didn't know before
# you
## made it

Mistakes are not a good way of learning anything

# It is better to
# have a
## little idea about a big thing
# than a
## big idea about a little thing

Pettiness is one of the most
self-destructive traits imaginable

# If you step back, your enemy will think you are going to strike

You are the choreographer of your own life

# If the blade is blunt, stab

As you do your work, be aware that a tool isn't broken until it won't do the job

# Madness is
# not
# measured
# by weight

Quantify only with appropriate measurements

# Your weapon does not know your skill

If you are relying on someone to know something, make sure they do

# Its reflection can be as desirable as the thing

Look carefully at what you are trying to achieve.
Does it remain unchanged? Look hard!

# Leave
## regrets where
# you
# find them

It is hard, but an essential ability
must be to control harmful emotions

# The chance of chance existing is zero

Plan your most productive accidents

# A simile is just
# like
# a simile

Identifying unproductive activity
is a continuous, passionate crusade

# Stare hard
# at the
# fog

If something is stopping you from seeing your goal,
stare at that instead

# Empty the cup before you ask for it to be filled again

Use the resources you have
not the ones you have been promised

# People spend their whole lives trying to buy what they already own

If the act of buying is the pleasure, you don't need what you are buying

# Talking leaves
# no
# trace

Always remember the words that you need
to quote again with precise accuracy

# Praise as you are

**leaving; complain upon arrival**

Do not store up complaints
waiting for the right time to say them

# If you break a leg it is an accident; if you land well it is a leap

Sometimes avoiding risk is more dangerous than accepting it

# Celebrate
## with a piss, commiserate
# with
# a banquet

For selfish reasons, always treat those who fail as if they had achieved great success

# You are never wearing your armour when the enemy attacks unless you wear it all the time

Career armour is the heaviest and most restricting. Only wear the elements you need

# Knowing is not the same as understanding

Know as little as possible.
Understand well the little you know

# Whilst the bomb is ticking, it is safe

Be aware of situations that could explode and those that are benign

# The letter after

# X

The crucial questions
are the secret of success

# If you want to know

# if a

# film is interesting,

# watch it

# standing up

Judge theories using practical tests

# New scenery cannot change

# old eyes

Never rely on novelty
to produce a good result

# If they bounce, they are dead

Accept without question what can be seen to be obviously true and do not speak about it

# Reverse is
## forward if that's
# the
## way you want to go

Ignore labels; they are about the past,
the way things were. If necessary, invent
a whole new vocabulary for your world

# The ground
## does not choose the weeds
# that grow
# on it

Do not waste time on the things that are
out of your control, and do not control
the things you can just for the sake of it

# The hungry are the worst hunters

## worst hunters

Be sure that your need to succeed
does not become the reason for action

# If it lives in the dark
# you
# don't want
# to see it

*Focus energy on what you know
has to be done*

# Learn to
## eat locusts
# and
## you will never
## be hungry

Be quick to do the tasks
that others do not want to do

# If you have a
## fallback position, you
# will
# use it

*A plan is not a static point,
it is a series of points in time*

# No man's
# land
## belongs to someone

Do not deny ownership of any part of a project just because it went wrong

# A plan
## is not a list
# of
## desired outcomes

Not all the ingredients in a recipe will taste good,
but together they can be perfect

# You

## can ignore knowledge
## but you cannot ignore
# ignorance

Study carefully the stupid words and actions
of stupid people. It is essential to know
what motivates the truly daft

# Always carry one

## or three arrows, never two

Confidence is felt when resources
are known to match the task

# Revenge should be treated like any other attack

You cannot choose to feel nothing, therefore you might as well select the most useful emotion

# Fear is only
## an approximate gauge
# of a
# situation

Even in extreme states of excitement, rational logic based on observations is still the best asset

# A dog has no record of who it

# has

# bitten

Do not ask those you are sure do not know
the answer you are seeking

# Record your victories as you would record defeats

Remember, one day you will look back on the history of current events

# Do not
## learn from failure, learn
# from
# success

Only intervene when you can use
experience from a previous success

# Mathematics is the best weapon of all

Being able to make accurate predictions
is a rare luxury.
Enjoy them to the full when you can

# A warning shot must be as carefully aimed as any other

When planning, do not exclude things just because the outcome is certain

# Being lied to is a compliment

## is a compliment

Assemble information
and treat it all with equal caution

# It is better to be without a weapon
## without a weapon
# than
## to share one

Waiting is a very good option when planning

# The
# closer
## you can hide to your hunter,
## the less likely they
## are to find you

Expectations must be managed as tightly
as any other element in a project

# Chase realities
# not
# dreams

Anything is capable of being achieved
with enough planned steps.
Twenty little steps are easier than five big ones.

# Treat necessities
# as
# luxuries

Venerate the commonplace.
Worship the ordinary

# Happiness is only ever a stowaway **on** other feelings

The pleasure that comes from the completion of a well-executed project is unique

# A void can go unnoticed

Your enemies are always busier than your friends

# Assassins do not get paid for effort

Clearly identify the rewards expected by others

# Why
## predict what you
# do not
## need to know?

Just because a task appears productive
doesn't mean that it is

# The only way to find seeds in the desert is to water the sand

Innovation in solving problems is one of the most valuable skills

# You
## cannot
### know how you know

Avoid unnecessary analysis and research
that simply gives you what you didn't need to know

# What
# do you
## need distracting from?

The highest-reward tasks
are often the least obvious

# Only illuminate what you want to see

Make sure you are in control of
all the information sources you have.
More information is not better information

# You cannot learn your
# way
## out of ignorance

No knowledge is better
than inaccurate knowledge

# If you feel homesick

# when

## you are at home,

# it is

# loneliness

A word is not a feeling.
A word is the name of a feeling

# Why are you hanging around when it's already left town?

Be constantly vigilant
for where the action really is

# Insignificance is the
# best
# hiding place

Practise being the least
noticed person in a room

# Leave it on the beach

Invent a place in your head
where you leave everything you don't need

# What is easy is

# not

## necessarily
## worthless

Do not grade the value of a task
by how hard it is

# Say 'cow' think 'sheep'

Never forget that words are not things

# You are the

## ferry you are waiting
## for downstream

Leave what you will need in the future
on the river bank so it is waiting for you
when you get there

# Dying is easy, it's from then on that it gets difficult

The order of things is not fixed.
Many fewer events are
absolutely fixed in time than you think

# People who say they
# are
# moving on,
# rarely do

Make no comment about yourself
that does not contain information needed
by the person you are speaking to

# Pointless is a reason

Do not discriminate between pointless and meaningful, big and trivial. Undertake all tasks with all of you

# You
## aren't doing nothing, you are waiting

Meditate on the idea of nothing
until the waiting ends

# The
## longer you have nothing
# the
## more valuable it becomes

Wear a blindfold and ask someone to drive you
to a part of town you do not know and drop you
in an unfamiliar suburban street.
Walk until you recognise where you are

# Realisation
# is
# innovation

Lightning strikes have to be encouraged
with conductors as high up as possible

# Everything aspires
# to be
# ordinary

If you do not prevent it, even the most seemingly
unusual things will slowly become mundane

# The way to achieve
# it is
## not to try to achieve it

Big is not important. All the little things that make up big are the most important

# Torment is in the eyes, anger in the mouth

Look in the mirror
and turn yourself into a stranger

# Enough is always **an** unknown quantity

Sit quietly in silence. In one way it is everything, in another it is nothing. Both are of equal value